Gerald R. Ford

Presidential Perspectives from the National Archives

National Archives and Records Administration
Washington, DC

PUBLISHED FOR THE
NATIONAL ARCHIVES AND RECORDS ADMINISTRATION
BY THE NATIONAL ARCHIVES TRUST FUND BOARD
1994

Library of Congress Cataloging-in-Publication Data

Gerald R. Ford.
p. cm.—(Presidential perspectives from the National Archives.)
Includes bibliographical references (p.).
ISBN 1-880875-04-7
1. Ford, Gerald R., 1913– . 2. Presidents—United States—Biography. 3. Gerald R. Ford Library. 4. Presidents—United States—History. I. United States. National Archives and Records Administration. II. Series.
E866.G47 1994
973.925'092–dc20
[B] 94-27162
CIP

Frank H. Mackaman wrote the biography of Gerald Ford and the entry for the Gerald R. Ford Foundation. Leesa Tobin composed the section on Betty Ford. David Horrocks wrote the Ford Library and Museum sections. The Presidential historical perspective is based on text in *The Presidents* (National Park Service, 1977), edited by Robert G. Ferris and James H. Charleton and revised by Lewis L. Gould. Photographs were selected by Ken Hafeli from the collections of the Gerald R. Ford Library. Edited by Henry J. Gwiazda and Janel McCarthy and designed by Serene Feldman Werblood.

All photographs are from the collections of the Gerald R. Ford Library unless otherwise noted.

OPPOSITE: President Ford and his golden retriever, Liberty, share a quiet moment in the Oval Office.

Gerald R. Ford
Thirty-eighth President
1974–77

When Richard Nixon resigned the Presidency in late summer 1974, Gerald Ford assumed the leadership of a country in turmoil. Ford had not sought the Oval Office. He came to it reluctantly under the terms of the 25th amendment, the first President to do so. Denied an electoral mandate and the customary transition to name advisers and plan a legislative program, the new President had to improvise.

"The State of the Union is not good," observed Ford in his first full report to Congress. The worst inflation in peacetime history ravaged the hopes and incomes of millions of Americans. Compounded by fears of an energy crisis, the worst recession in a generation would soon plague the economy. A long and divisive war in Southeast Asia dragged on, and allies questioned the United States' resolve. Perhaps most important of all, many Americans had lost confidence in the integrity of their political leaders. Watergate had traumatized the public and paralyzed the government. Although Ford had served in Congress for 25 years and as Vice President for 8 months, the country did not know their new President well.

ABOVE: *Bureau of Engraving and Printing*

RIGHT: Betty Ford holds the bible on which her husband has just taken the Presidential oath of office in August 1974.

National Park Service (Special Collection)

Dorothy Gardner King holds her young son, Leslie L. King, Jr., in 1913. As a young boy, Leslie would take the name of his stepfather, Gerald Rudolph Ford.

Gerald Rudolph Ford was born on July 14, 1913, in Omaha, NE. He was christened Leslie L. King, Jr., after his father, a wool dealer. His parents' marriage soon failed, however, and his mother, Dorothy Gardner, moved with her young son to Grand Rapids, MI, her family's home. She remarried the following year. Her new husband, Gerald R. Ford, a paint salesman, informally adopted young Leslie and gave him his own name. Ford recalled his stepfather as "a marvelous family man." Although his parents were of modest means, "emotionally both were very secure," Ford continued, "and if I retain that characteristic today, I owe it to them." Three half brothers eventually joined the Ford household, forming a tightly knit family where Gerald R. Ford, Jr., learned the value of hard work and discipline, virtues that would serve him well in the years to come.

Ford attended the public schools of Grand Rapids. He received average grades for the courses he disliked (Latin, for example), but generally he excelled, ranking in the top 5 percent of his 220-member South High class. As center and team captain for the school's football team, he emerged a local hero and began a treasured, lifelong association with athletics. Ford explained his interest in these words: "Athletics, my parents kept saying, built a boy's character." Ford worked part-time during school grilling hamburgers, washing dishes, and manning the cash register at a popular restaurant across from South High. During vacations, he worked in the senior Ford's small paint manufacturing company. Ford attributed a fundamental part of his philosophy to these teenage years:

> *Everyone, I decided, had more good qualities than bad. If I understood and tried to accentuate those good qualities in others, I could get along much better. Hating or even disliking people because of their bad qualities, it seemed to me, was a waste of time.*

Ford poses with his half brothers Tom, Dick, and Jim and his stepfather, Gerald, in 1927. Within the close Ford family, the future President learned the value of hard work and discipline.

To help pay for his Yale law degree, Ford joined the university's athletic staff as an assistant coach for football and boxing. He was photographed in 1938 with two other assistant football coaches, Jim DeAngelis and "Ivy" Williamson.

After graduating from high school in 1931, Ford enrolled in the University of Michigan, where he majored in economics and political science. He had to bus tables at the university hospital and wash dishes in a fraternity house to support himself. He donated blood every 2 or 3 months for $25, one-fourth the annual tuition. Even with this demanding schedule, Ford earned a "B" average in his classes and still found time to play football. The backup center on Michigan's national championship teams in 1932 and 1933, by his senior year Ford started at center and was named the team's most valuable player. In 1935, the year of his graduation, he played in the College All-Star Game.

Despite offers from the Detroit Lions and the Green Bay Packers to play professional ball, Ford had decided that "pro football wouldn't lead me anywhere." The law, where Ford could employ his talents as mediator and counselor, held considerably more appeal. Lack of money still posed a problem, but Ford found the solution again in sports. He joined the athletic staff at Yale University, working as an assistant football and boxing coach while he attended Yale Law School. In 1941, finishing in the top third of his class, Ford received his law degree. Among his fellow students were Cyrus Vance, Potter Stewart, and Sargent Shriver.

After gaining admission to the Michigan bar, Ford practiced law in Grand Rapids until World War II cut the experience short. Following Pearl Harbor, he enlisted in the Navy as an ensign and spent a substantial part of his tour of duty as an operations officer on the aircraft carrier U.S.S. *Monterey* in the Pacific. His captain described him as "steady, reliable, and resourceful," possessed of "natural ability as a leader," and popular with his men. Ford left the Navy in 1946 with the rank of lieutenant commander. More important for his political future, Ford's wartime experiences gave him "an entirely new perspective" on world affairs. Ford became an ardent internationalist and unswerving supporter of military preparedness—two principles that guided him throughout his public service.

Ford resumed his law career upon his return to Grand Rapids. In 1948 he married Elizabeth (Betty) Bloomer Warren, a department store fashion coordinator and a former dancer in the Martha Graham Concert Group. The Fords were to have three sons and one daughter: Michael, John, Steven, and Susan.

In 1948 Ford not only married but also entered the political arena. The incumbent congressman in the district was an isolationist Republican. Ford's stepfather, a local Republican leader, and Michigan Senator Arthur H. Vandenberg, a spokesman for a bipartisan internationalist foreign policy, were looking for a young challenger to oust the incumbent. They encouraged Ford to enter the race, and he won the Republican primary in a political upset. In

During his World War II duty as assistant navigator aboard the U.S.S. *Monterey* in the Pacific, Ford takes a sextant reading.

On October 15, 1948, having resumed his law career, Gerald Ford married Elizabeth Bloomer Warren, a department store fashion coordinator and former dancer.

solidly Republican west Michigan, he easily won the general election.

Close attention to his constituents resulted in 12 reelections for Ford, usually with more than 60 percent of the vote. He rose quietly within his party's leadership during 25 years in the House of Representatives (1949–73) by advancing Republican policies, playing a key role on the Defense Appropriations Subcommittee, and working assiduously in party affairs. His colleagues recognized his skill and contributions by electing him minority leader during the last 8 years of his tenure.

Ford was one of the most respected and popular members of the House on both sides of the aisle. Early in 1973, however, he and Mrs. Ford discussed his retirement plans. Reluctantly, he had concluded that he would never attain his major political ambition, to be Speaker of the House. They agreed that Ford would run one more time in 1974 and retire from public life after that term, when he would be 63 years old and young enough to begin another career. Within months, circumstances conspired to change their plans.

During the autumn of 1973, Vice President Spiro Agnew resigned. President Nixon considered John Connally, Nelson Rockefeller, and Ronald Reagan before settling on Ford to nominate as Vice President, believing that Ford faced the fewest obstacles to confirmation. The Congress held extensive hearings on Ford's qualifications, and then both branches gave him an overwhelmingly favorable vote of confirmation in December. Eight months later, on August 9, 1974, Nixon resigned, and Gerald Ford was inaugurated as the 38th President. "My fellow Americans, our long national nightmare is over," Ford intoned as he asked for the nation's prayers.

The new President was a product of mainstream American institutions—his church, team sports, the military, the law, the Republican party, and Congress. These

Congressman Ford speaks with residents of Hudsonville, MI, outside his mobile office in September 1955. The office exemplified Ford's determination to remain in close touch with his constituents.

Ford meets with Vice President Nelson Rockefeller and Cabinet members on July 20, 1976. Ford took great pride in the high quality of his appointments to the Cabinet, the Supreme Court, and major commissions.

influences formed his approach to governing the nation. He had learned in these experiences the value of leadership by consensus:

> *I have spent my whole life trying to pull people together. I've always tried to create a team environment, whether it was in athletics, on board ship in the navy, or in politics. I think that's the only way to get the job done.*

In sharp contrast to Nixon, Ford opened up his administration, abolishing many of the ceremonial trappings of the so-called "Imperial Presidency." He traveled and met with people extensively, speaking publicly an average of 43 times per month. Although criticized for a certain blandness in public appearances, Ford keenly felt the importance of presenting himself to the people. In 1976, for example, he delivered 682 speeches, or one every 6 hours assuming a 12-hour work day, a rate not even surpassed by Ronald Reagan, the Great Communicator. Ford considered this public contact among his most important functions. "[We] dissipated the angry attitude that people had toward government and toward one another," Ford once responded when asked about his greatest achievement.

As Ford tried to reconnect the Presidency to the American people, he took other actions to restore the integrity of government. Two weeks after assuming office, he announced a program by which

On September 8, 1974, hoping to refocus the public on policy issues, Ford granted Richard Nixon a full pardon for all crimes he may have committed while in office. The plan backfired, and Ford's approval ratings plummeted.

draft evaders and deserters could earn amnesty. Later, Ford appointed a commission, headed by his Vice President, Nelson Rockefeller, to investigate and report on abuses of power by the American intelligence community. He supported the Attorney General in limiting investigative actions by the FBI. Finally, Ford took great pride in the high quality of his appointments to the Cabinet, the Supreme Court, and major commissions.

In his approach to public policy, Ford's political philosophy, best described as pragmatic conservatism, figured prominently. Ford believed that the real purpose of government was to enhance the lives of the people and that "a leader can best do that by restraining government in most cases instead of enlarging it at every opportunity." He endorsed traditional Republican principles: belief in the free enterprise system, support for a strong national defense, wide latitude for local and state governments to make their own decisions, and minimum government interference in business-labor relations and the conduct of individual lives. As Ford was wont to say, "A government big enough to give you everything you want is a government big enough to take from you everything you have."

Rescuing the public perception of the presidency loomed as Ford's central task. His bold first strike misfired badly. On September 8, 1974, 1 month after taking office, Ford granted Richard Nixon a full pardon for all crimes he may have committed during his Presidency. Ford hoped to engender a spirit of national reconciliation and to turn the nation's attention away from Watergate. He had miscalculated. "I thought there would be greater forgiveness," Ford lamented, "It was one of the greatest disappointments of my Presidency that everyone focused on the individual instead of on the problems the nation faced." The public's initial confidence in Ford plummeted, his approval ratings dropping from 71 to 49 percent

Ford meets with Egyptian President Anwar Sadat in Salzburg, Austria, on June 2, 1975.

During his administration, Ford pursued an active foreign policy. His November 1974 meeting with Soviet General Secretary Leonid Brezhnev in Vladivostok, U.S.S.R., laid the groundwork for a new long-term SALT agreement.

almost overnight. The new President never fully escaped the pardon's consequences.

During the balance of his term, Ford wrestled with a restive and overwhelmingly Democratic Congress to chart the country's course. He achieved mixed results. On the domestic front, Ford practiced pragmatic conservatism by using the veto aggressively to thwart congressional spending. During 2½ years in office, he vetoed 66 bills—only 12 were overridden. He estimated that these vetoes reduced the rate of growth in government spending by half, saving each household $150 annually.

Ford spent considerable energy attacking the country's poor economic performance. In his first State of the Union message, he proposed a 1-year moratorium on new federal spending, a $16-billion temporary tax reduction, a series of energy and conservation taxes and fees, and a permanent tax reduction to return these taxes and fees to the economy. Later, he sought tax reform measures and regulatory reform legislation in the transportation, energy, banking, and retail industries. Ford's actions had some effect: Inflation fell by more than half, and post-recession employment increased by 3.5 million jobs. But the economy bedeviled the administration, and Ford has since admitted that continued economic difficulties and unemployment were his greatest frustration. Having grown up during the Depression, Ford found these problems particularly poignant: "I understood the problems from personal experience, and, yet, there was nothing I could do instantaneously to change it."

The lack of time and his conservative nature limited Ford's activism. Still, by August 1976, it took 75 pages for his staff to describe the accomplishments of Ford's abbreviated Presidency. Among those often overlooked were Ford's support of the Housing and Community Development Act, which prohibited discrimination on the basis of sex in housing and mortgage lending. He also signed the Equal Credit

Ford campaigns in Walnut Creek, CA, in May 1976. Despite a vigorous campaign, Ford was unable to regain the confidence of the American people and so lost the election to Democrat Jimmy Carter.

Opportunity Act barring discrimination against consumers by creditors. He favored and signed the Military Procurement Bill of 1975, which permitted the admission of women to the service academies. He ratified bills to aid education and to regulate campaign practices. He signed the Safe Drinking Water Act to establish and enforce national drinking water standards. Six of his proposals for dealing with the energy crisis received congressional approval. He established an Office of Science and Technology Policy in the White House.

Although considerably more experienced on the domestic side, Ford did not neglect foreign policy. Working with such tough-minded and realistic Western leaders as Helmut Schmidt of West Germany, Valéry Giscard d'Estaing of France, and James Callaghan of Great Britain, Ford sought an active role for the United States. He had summits with his allied colleagues more than 60 times—including two summits with NATO leaders in 1975 and economic summits at Rambouillet, France, and at Dorado Beach, Puerto Rico. He negotiated the Vladivostok Agreement in 1974 with the Soviet Union, which broke a 2½ year deadlock and laid the groundwork for a new long-term SALT (strategic arms limitation talks) agreement. In October 1975, with considerable assistance from the Ford administration, Israel and Egypt reached an interim peace accord, the first Arab-Israeli agreement that was not the immediate result of hostilities. At the Helsinki Conference, the President declared publicly to the Soviet communist leadership that America insisted on human rights, self-determination, and freer movement of peoples and ideas as the true basis for security in Europe and throughout the world. Ford successfully reversed a 10-year trend of congressional cutbacks in the nation's defense strength and reorganized the nation's intelligence assets to enhance their effectiveness.

When Ford left office in 1977, no American was engaged in battle, a first in a decade. American military forces, where they had been used during Ford's Presidency, were used to save lives—to save Americans and Vietnamese fleeing from Indochina after the collapse of Saigon in April 1975, to rescue the ship and crew of the *Mayaguez* seized by Cambodians a month later, and to save the lives of Americans in Lebanon.

Despite his efforts and concrete accomplishments, Ford did not inspire the American people. He earned their respect, even affection, but he did not command their confidence. On the eve of his campaign for the Presidency, 61 percent of Americans could not name anything Ford had done to impress them. Nevertheless, Ford beat back a vigorous challenge from Ronald Reagan for the Republican nomination. "To me, the Presidency and the Vice-Presidency were not prizes to be won, but a duty to be done," Ford told the audience at the nominating convention in Kansas

CIA Director George Bush points out to President Ford possible evacuation routes for Americans from Beirut, Lebanon, during a National Security Council meeting on June 17, 1976.

In September 1976 President Ford and Jimmy Carter debate domestic policy at the Walnut Street Theater in Philadelphia during the first of three Presidential campaign debates.

City. "[It] is not the power and glamour of the Presidency that leads me to ask for another 4 years; it is something every hard-working American will understand—the challenge of a job well begun, but far from finished." Ford and his Vice-Presidential running mate, Senator Robert Dole of Kansas, began well behind the Democratic ticket of Jimmy Carter and Walter Mondale. Ford's energetic campaign closed the gap by election day, but in the end, it was not enough to win. The margin in the Electoral College was 297 votes for Carter to 241 for Ford; fewer than 2 million popular votes separated the two men.

The Fords retired to Palm Springs, CA, and the former President did not spend much time looking back. "I have competed enough in life and, whether it is athletics or politics or law, I know that sometimes you win and sometimes you lose," he recalled 10 years later. "I do not like to live in the past. The attitude that out of disappointment comes new opportunity has guided me in the years since 1977." In 1979 his autobiography, *A Time to Heal*, was published. He established the American Enterprise Institute World Forum in 1982, an annual meeting of world leaders and business executives he continues to host. He has spoken on nearly 200 campuses since leaving office, participates actively in the programs of the Gerald R. Ford Foundation, serves on several corporate boards, works on behalf of numerous charities, and speaks out for Republican candidates.

The substantive accomplishments of the Ford administration were necessarily modest, given the limited time in which he had to work and the turmoil of the mid-1970s. Ford reacted to what he thought people expected of the President, and he could see stark evidence of their cynicism and distrust of government. He responded not with boldness but with restraint, restraint in policy initiatives, and restraint in the use of Presidential powers. But Ford may have misunderstood the public's conflicting expectations of a President. The evidence is unclear on this point, but for many people, if not most, the solution to poor performance by government is more vigorous leadership, especially from the President.

President and Mrs. Ford comfort each other as they watch the election returns on November 2, 1976.

Ford's commitment to limits, however, made it impossible for him to quench Americans' thirst for "vision" from their President. "Too often 'vision' is just a fancy word people use to justify spending a lot of money," Ford once told an interviewer in a revealing comment. "You can spend an awful lot of money on some pretty unattainable goals. I'm more concerned with the nuts and bolts of getting from here to there."

He may have lacked a compelling vision, but ultimately, Ford's strength of character produced his Presidency's most lasting legacy for American politics. After the trauma of Watergate, Ford gave a sense of decency and pride back to the Oval Office. His personal integrity, his self-confidence, his emotional balance, his civility, and his industry restored the Presidency. By virtue of who he was and the way he conducted himself, Gerald Ford rescued the American Presidency at a time of crisis. In the words of the *New York Times* as Ford was about to leave office:

> *Mr. Ford today enjoys the respect and affection of his fellow citizens. Moreover, he leaves the country in better shape than he found it. Those two achievements may seem modest, but they eluded several of his more brilliant predecessors. Mr. Ford has a right to take satisfaction from them.*

Betty Ford

After taking the oath of office on August 9, 1974, the new President's first public statement included the following testimonial: "I am indebted to no man, and only to one woman—my dear wife . . ." It was an acknowledgement of the extraordinary public and private partnership of Gerald and Betty Ford.

Elizabeth Ann Bloomer was born April 8, 1918. She grew up in Grand Rapids and, after a stint with the Martha Graham Concert Group, returned to support herself as the fashion coordinator for a local department store. After a brief first marriage ended in divorce, she began dating "the most eligible bachelor in Grand Rapids."

In February 1948, Jerry Ford offered her this mysterious proposal: "I'd like to marry you," he said. "But we can't get married until next fall, and I can't tell you why." The reasons for the delay and the secrecy lay in his first campaign for the U.S. House of Representatives. Two weeks after their wedding, Jerry Ford was elected to Congress, and Betty Ford's life as a political wife began.

As a model congressional spouse and mother of four children, Mrs. Ford ran the household, joined women's clubs, taught Sunday school, attended political functions, and escorted visiting constituents around Washington. She found herself often without her increasingly prominent husband. During the busiest of years, Minority Leader Ford was away from home 258 days.

In 1973, at a time when Mrs. Ford looked forward to a quiet retirement and spending more time with her husband, she was swept up in the events of Watergate and found herself the most scrutinized woman in America. Now a public figure in her own right, she rose to the occasion. Her warmth, good humor, and penchant for straight talk reassured Americans that the White House was no longer a fortress but the residence of a family with whom they could identify.

As First Lady, Mrs. Ford won respect and admiration for her frankness about subjects ranging from breast cancer and premarital sex to equal rights for women. At times her opinions diverged from those of her husband and generated public debate over

LEFT: While Betty Ford's controversial August 1975 "60 Minutes" interview with Morley Safer earned her criticism from some, many Americans were impressed by her frankness in expressing opinions that sometimes diverged from those of the President.

BELOW: In the weeks following her mastectomy in September 1974, Betty Ford received more than 50,000 cards and messages of good will—many from women who had undergone similar operations.

the proper role of a First Lady. Her controversial "60 Minutes" interview in August 1975, for example, triggered a deluge of nearly 35,000 letters and telegrams, many of them critical. Yet she pleased far more people than she offended. Several months after the interview, a Harris Poll found that Mrs. Ford had become one of history's most popular First Ladies and an asset to her husband in the 1976 Presidential campaign.

She put her popularity to work in an aggressive effort to persuade state legislators across the country to approve the Equal Rights Amendment. Forthright about her own experience with breast cancer, she used her position to alert women to the benefits of early detection. These experiences revealed the influence and power she could wield as First Lady—"Not my power," as she put it later, "but the power of the position, a power which could be used to help."

After her family left the White House, candor remained her trademark. She went public with her decision to seek professional help for prescription drug and alcohol dependence, which she chronicled in her books, *Betty Ford: The Times of My Life*, and *Betty: A Glad Awakening*. During the first few years of her recovery, Mrs. Ford worked tirelessly to establish the Betty Ford Center at the Eisenhower Medical Center in southern California. As president of the center, she is still very much involved in its daily operations and speaks often about alcoholism treatment to groups throughout the country. In 1991 she became only the third First Lady to appear before Congress when she testified on the subject before a subcommittee of the House of Representatives. Mrs. Ford remains active in other fields as well. She continues to work with the American Cancer Society on breast cancer awareness and participates in fund-raising efforts for AIDS research and the National Arthritis Foundation.

In the words of Edith Mayo, curator of the First Ladies exhibit at the Smithsonian Institution, "Betty Ford helped restore the public's faith in the Presidency as an institution by creating an atmosphere of honesty." In one of the most difficult of public roles, Betty Ford had the courage to develop her own voice. During a time when women's traditional roles were being questioned, she reassured Americans that feminism and families were not incompatible. And she proved that she could not only overcome life-threatening problems herself, but she could also help others find the will to do the same.

In the presence of his wife, President Ford signs a proclamation declaring 1975 International Women's Year. In Betty Ford, American women found a strong advocate of equal rights.

Built on the Ann Arbor campus of the University of Michigan, the Gerald R. Ford Library contains nearly 20 million historical papers and audiovisuals documenting Ford's life and career.

The Gerald R. Ford Library and Museum

Former President Ford addresses guests at the dedication of the Gerald R. Ford Museum in Grand Rapids, MI, on September 17, 1981.

The Gerald R. Ford Library and Museum are separated by 130 miles but joined in a common program under one director. The library/archives is on the Ann Arbor campus of the University of Michigan, Ford's 1935 alma mater. The museum overlooks a city park on the Grand River in Grand Rapids, MI, where Ford grew to adulthood and won repeated election to Congress.

The separation is unique among the nation's Presidential libraries. It is a compromise between competing claims on Ford's loyalties and affections, certainly, but the split location is an experiment as well. The experiment is in the use of two sites to better accomplish the twin missions of every Presidential library. A museum excites interest and learning about American history and public affairs through exhibits and other popular programs. Nearly 40 million people have visited Presidential museums over the years. An archives, by contrast, provides the raw information that people need to interpret their past, chart their future, and hold their government accountable. Although millions benefit indirectly when archival material is distilled into books, news stories, and television programs, an archives is by nature a place for quiet analysis.

Both buildings were built with private funds and opened to the public in 1981. The National Archives maintains the buildings and runs the programs, but it relies on the Gerald R. Ford Foundation and other partners to fund special programs such as research grants and new exhibits.

The Library in Ann Arbor

The Ford Library's research room seats only 15 at full capacity, but the patrons are surprisingly diverse, as a recent autumn illustrated. Scholars from Britain, Canada, Israel, and Germany photocopied stacks of documents to carry home for analysis. While graduate students cast hesitantly for material on the Turkish invasion of Cyprus or agricultural price supports, a former Director of Central Intelligence zeroed in on

Scholars, students, and patrons examine documents in the library's research room.

specific files for his memoirs. A journalist examined files that helped him explain would-be assassin Lynette "Squeaky" Fromme as an icon for the failure of 1960s social protest.

Not all of the autumn researchers were writing books, articles, and papers. Memorandums on the space program pleased a local engineer on an extended lunch hour, and dozens of wary undergraduates filtered in and out to complete a 3-hour archival exercise for their class, "Information Sources for the Mass Media." The Ford Library's director, meanwhile, led a semester-long political science seminar on the various ways Presidents organize and manage their staffs.

Many people use the library without setting foot in it. By the end of a given year, archivists will have answered over a thousand requests for information or reproductions from callers and correspondents all over the world. The queries will have come from magazine and television production staffs, the White House and Congress, public schools and private homes, renowned institutions, and earnest doctoral students.

The focus of these interests is nearly 20 million original historical paper and audiovisual items—option memorandums, meet ing minutes, campaign plans, telephone notes, correspondence, photographs, films, videotapes, and more. There is even a long telegram on economic policy from a then-obscure and unsuccessful Arkansas congressional candidate, Bill Clinton. Most of the material, enough to fill several moving vans, was written or received by the hundreds of men and women who worked in the Ford White House complex between 1974 and 1977. Other material dates from Ford's long career in Congress and brief term as Vice President.

Starting in 1977 and continuing to the present, Ford Library staff have added millions of pages of related material, often donated by individuals who value the way history enriches the future. The library shelves have gained such material as an unpublished memoir of human rights policy, dozens of research interviews, and a private diary of the Nixon-Ford transition.

The result is an immense information trove on the 1970s, a decade rich in drama and consequence. A generation of domestic politics echoes from the resignation of Richard Nixon, the post-Watergate assertiveness of Congress and the press, Ronald Reagan's run for the 1976 Republican nomination, and Ford's appointments of George Bush as envoy to China and then as Director of Central Intelligence. The vivid collapse of Saigon, the Helsinki Accords on human rights and national boundaries in Eastern Europe, and the shock of the Arab oil embargo helped shape foreign policy for years to come. Mrs. Ford's support of the Equal Rights Amendment or President Ford's war-by-veto against federal spending prefigured social and economic issues of later years.

The library is more than a place for storing 20 million documents and seating those who would read them. The library is really a bundle of programs designed to make the gargantuan mass of paper and film truly accessible. Archivists provide expert advice and practical assistance in finding information that people want, and nothing illustrates this better than PRESNET. An automated database with a precision that is unsurpassed in the archival profession, PRESNET describes about 50,000 folder titles of historical material, helping the public quickly locate material on any topic.

Description and reference, however, come only after a long process. Archivists first locate, acquire, and organize materials. Archivists also find and temporarily restrict certain kinds of information—national security classified and investigative information, for example, or material that could clearly cause an invasion of an individual's privacy. These decisions can be highly controversial, and the review process takes a large chunk of staff time.

The sensitivity and complexity of "archival processing" require archivists to

master the history of the period. They study the politics, policies, and the policy-makers. At the Ford Library, different staff members concentrate on such tasks as acquisitions, preservation, security declassification, automated systems, audiovisual materials, reference, and teaching.

These activities take place in an attractive building on the University of Michigan's North Campus, a sort of suburban annex linked by frequent commuter buses to the Central Campus in downtown Ann Arbor. A low-lying brick and bronze-tinted glass structure with abundant natural lighting and oak trim, it has proven a pleasant and functional home since 1980.

The library is devoted first to the care and use of its historical materials, but its attractive lobby and auditorium spaces make it a popular site for small-scale academic events and public programs co-sponsored by the Gerald R. Ford Foundation and other groups. Although the library hosts a variety of events each year, the focus of public programming is at the Museum in Grand Rapids, MI.

TOP: Before taping the library's televised conference "The Presidency and the Constitution," moderator Fred Friendly warms up the panel, which included (*left to right*) Attorney General Edwin Meese, Dan Rather, Gary Sick, Stansfield Turner, and Representative Dick Cheney.

BOTTOM: Library Director Frank Mackaman teaches a class on the 1976 campaign to University of Michigan honor students. Undergraduates compose the majority of the library's patrons.

LEFT: The Gerald R. Ford Museum was built in Grand Rapids, MI, where Ford grew to adulthood.

BELOW: "Presidential Pets," another of the museum's exhibits, proved popular with visitors.

ABOVE LEFT: A display in the museum recalls the Quonset hut that served as Ford's first campaign headquarters in 1948.

ABOVE RIGHT: The exhibit "Entertaining in Style" provides a glimpse into White House social events.

The Museum in Grand Rapids

The Ford Museum is a granite and glass triangular structure overlooking the Grand River and connected by footbridge and street with Grand Rapids's prospering downtown and conference center. The museum is a short walk from the site of Ford's first campaign headquarters. There, in 1948, the young World War II veteran challenged an isolationist incumbent for the Republican congressional nomination. The headquarters was a military-style Quonset hut that bespoke a victorious generation's awareness that America was a world power with world responsibilities.

That 1948 headquarters, with the haphazard furnishings and flyers of a volunteer operation, is remembered in a Ford Museum display. An exhibit gallery away, visitors walk through Ford's last political headquarters. It is the White House Oval Office in 1976, exactly replicated and given authenticity by many original artifacts. In these two spaces and in the exhibit galleries around them, museum visitors experience the drama of American political history since World War II.

Where the library offers an analytic approach to our past and our government, the museum provokes emotions that stimulate learning and reflection at a later moment. For some older visitors, the emotion may be the catharsis of reliving moments of national pain or pride. For others, the emotion is the wonder of time travel and the curiosity that can follow. For everyone, as they stand in the Oval Office or walk among the artifacts and read their stories, the museum evokes a third response—a sense of democratic citizenship. The Presidency is theirs to see and touch (almost), to use, and to hold accountable.

A Ford Museum visit begins with a half-hour award-winning film that introduces exhibit themes and infuses them with the faces and voices of the past. Those who witnessed the wrenching end to the Vietnam war, or the majesty of the Tall Ships in New York's harbor on the nation's 200th birthday, can feel old but unforgotten emotions and, perhaps, share them

Eleanor Seagraves, granddaughter of Franklin D. Roosevelt, recalls her life in the White House during the "Modern First Ladies, Private Lives, and Public Duties" conference held at the museum in April 1984. Luci Johnson Turpin, Susan Ford Vance, Rosalyn Carter, Betty Ford, and Linda Johnson Robb also participated.

with a child or grandchild. The trauma of Watergate is there, too, and provides the basis for the film's title, "The Presidency Restored." Later, in the exhibit areas near the Oval Office, visitors scan across Congressman Ford's desktop on October 10, 1973, the day Richard Nixon selected Ford to become Vice President. On the desk in eloquent irony, amid Ford's keepsakes and paperwork, is a personal note from disgraced Vice President Spiro Agnew, telling Ford of his intention to resign.

Some visitors are more taken by the glamour of the Presidency. Who among us could decline attending a state dinner for the President of France? At the museum one joins the table of President d'Estaing, Mrs. Ford, actor Clint Eastwood, and dance pioneer Martha Graham. The White House china, crystal, and silver, the name card calligraphy, the carefully selected decoration—all recall an evening to remember.

Head of state gifts are as much a part of the ceremonial Presidency as state dinners, and many are superb examples of national craftsmanship. A 3-foot-high Waterford crystal vase, presented to Ford by Irish Prime Minister Liam Cosgrave, is a favorite among visitors. Others prefer the Sultan of Oman Qaboos Bin Said's gift. It is a diamond-crested gold falcon ready to soar from a silver perch. Taxpayers can be reassured that, under law, Presidents must register such gifts with the State Department as public property.

The permanent exhibits may be the core of the museum's program, but there is much more. Each year, a succession of temporary exhibits draws upon the rich holdings of the entire Presidential libraries system or the traveling exhibits offered by the Smithsonian Institution and others. For example, the National Archives' traveling exhibit "World War II: Personal Accounts" revealed the private experiences of war through the diaries, letters, photographs, and personal effects of over 100 combatants and civilians, plus some of their war leaders.

One of the many gifts on display at the museum is this autographed football given to the President in 1977.

Each year 15,000 to 20,000 people of all ages take advantage of a variety of special events organized by museum staff to supplement the exhibits. A 1940s fashion show attended by President and Mrs. Ford, a film series, and a guest lecture series supplemented the World War II exhibit. The museum's education specialist hosted a preview tour of the exhibit for social studies teachers who would bring their classes in large numbers. This constant renewal as well as priority attention to the needs of teachers and students are the reasons one school bus driver raved, "This is about the 50th or 60th time I've been here and this place still amazes me."

Not all museum programs revolve around the exhibits schedule. Many celebrate active citizenship. Each year, for example, high school students test their knowledge of public events in Citizens Bee competitions that originated as a local event and have grown to a national program. Other events range from periodic naturalization ceremonies for new citizens, attended by a few hundred, to the July 4th fireworks and festivities organized by the Grand Rapids community and enjoyed by tens of thousands from the museum grounds.

Future visitors to the Ford Museum have much to anticipate. New exhibits, better technology, changing public issues, and fresh interpretations will continuously renew the visitor experience. This experience will have, however, one constant. It is the power of historical documents and artifacts to stimulate thinking and learning through the stories of human drama they tell.

RIGHT: "Congress, the Presidency, and Foreign Policy" conferees Zbigniew Brezezinski, Alexander Haig, Dean Rusk, President Ford, William Rodgers, and Brent Scowcroft pose in Ford's private office at the library.

BELOW: Ford, flanked by Republican National Committee chairman Frank Fahrenkopf and Democratic National Committee chairman Paul Kirk, answers questions from the press during a 1985 conference on Presidential primaries.

The Gerald R. Ford Foundation

The ambitious educational and exhibition programs of the library and museum receive substantial financial support from the Gerald R. Ford Foundation, a nonprofit organization founded in 1981. The focus of the foundation is on conferences, symposia, research, and awards that improve public understanding of the challenges that confront government, and particularly the Presidency. Among its specific projects are:

- The Gerald R. Ford Colloquium, which has dealt with such diverse topics as German reunification, national security requirements in the 1990s, and the role of women in politics
- The research grants program, source of over $200,000 for more than 125 researchers who have made significant use of the Ford Library's collections in their work
- The Gerald R. Ford Journalism Prizes awarded annually for distinguished reporting on national defense issues and on the Presidency
- Support for temporary exhibitions at the museum on such topics as the Berlin Wall, political cartooning, the Bill of Rights, and the commemoration of World War II, among many others
- Conferences on revamping the Presidential nomination process, reducing the deficit through budget reform, the relationship between Congress and the Presidency on foreign policy, the role of the First Lady, the Social Security program, humor and the Presidency, and others
- Commemorative events, featuring foreign dignitaries and current government and political leaders
- Community enrichment programs, including Citizens Bees, film series, and teacher workshops.

In 1988 the foundation added the William E. Simon Lecture to its programs. Endowed by a gift to the Ford Foundation from Mr. Simon, who served as Secretary of the Treasury, the series hosts distinguished speakers who address a current issue in a public lecture. In 1993, for example, Mexican President Carlos Salinas de Gortari spoke before nearly 1,000 people at the University of Michigan on the importance of the North American Free Trade Agreement (NAFTA). In making his gift, Mr. Simon observed that "these lectures can make a significant, continuing contribution to public debate on how to preserve and strengthen the institutions of our free society."

Foundation programs reflect President Ford's strong interest in the work of the library and museum. They also recall his steadfast belief that private funding should be available for educational and public programs to complement the government-financed operation of the facilities.

Ford greets Carlos Salinas de Gortari before the Mexican President's 1993 speech on the benefits of the North American Free Trade Agreement (NAFTA). The Gerald R. Ford Foundation sponsored the address.

Before the opening of the museum's conference "Humor and the Presidency," Ford meets with comedian Chevy Chase, who frequently imitated the President.

Presidents Ford and Carter listen to David Mathews, former Secretary of Health, Education, and Welfare, during the Ford Library's 1983 conference on the public and public policy.

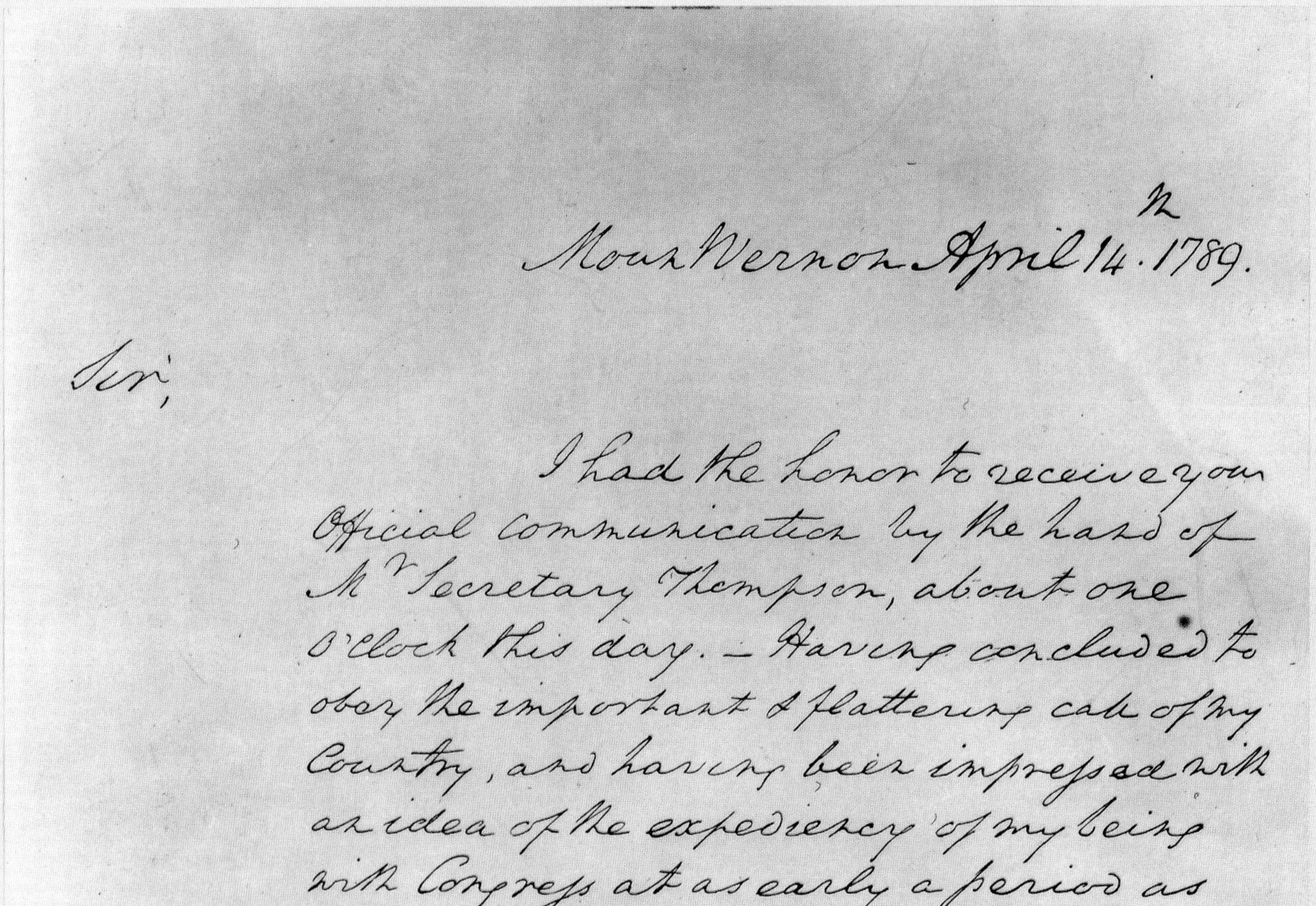

Mount Vernon April 14th 1789.

Sir;

I had the honor to receive your Official communication by the hand of Mr Secretary Thompson, about one O'clock this day. — Having concluded to obey the important & flattering call of my Country, and having been impressed with an idea of the expediency of my being with Congress at as early a period as possible; I propose to commence my journey on thursday morning which will be the day after to morrow. —

I have the honor to be
with sentiments of esteem
Sir
Your most Obedt Servt
Go: Washington

The Honble
Jno Langdon Esqr

With this April 1789 letter to John Langdon, George Washington accepted the Presidency, an office he did much to define.

Library of Congress

The Presidency in Historical Perspective

During the two centuries that the United States has functioned as a democracy, the institution of the Presidency has emerged as the central focus of the nation's political affairs. Through the crises that have confronted Americans over this period—a bitter civil war, world wars, economic depressions and panics, and major social upheavals—and in the moments of triumph and accomplishment, the Presidents have become the personification of what the United States stands for and seeks to be. The 40 men who have sat in the Oval Office thus represent an important source of continuity and confidence as citizens of the United States contemplate their government and its affairs.

The quality of the Presidents has been varied and often controversial. Some of them have been great men—Abraham Lincoln, George Washington, Franklin D. Roosevelt. Others have been failures and disappointments. Many have grown while in office; others fell short of demonstrating the qualities of character needed for Presidential success. The Presidency has usually defied simple generalizations and easy explanations about why some succeed in its duties and others fail.

The Presidency and the young United States of America did not seem destined for world leadership when the office was created during the 1787 Constitutional Convention. In 1789, when the Constitution went into effect, the nation was a small, rural, predominantly agricultural republic that consisted of 13 states along the eastern coast of North America. The population stood at 4 million people in a country that had virtually no weight in world affairs. Two centuries later, the United States has been transformed into an urban, industrial nation of 50 states extending westward to Alaska and Hawaii. The number of Americans stands near 260 million, and the country has become a superpower in economic, political, and military terms.

As the nation has grown, the institution of the Presidency has evolved with it. The 19th century was a time when the office expanded its powers somewhat, but a fundamental evolution of the modern Presidency began at the turn of the 20th century with the contributions of William McKinley, Theodore Roosevelt, and Woodrow Wilson. The emergence of the strong Presidency has taken place for a number of reasons. Faced with the chance to accomplish goals that were in the national interest, Presidents have turned to powers that were implied but not expressly stated in the Constitution. As both domestic and foreign demands on the government increased, Cabinet departments were expanded or newly established to meet these expanding requirements. Correspondingly, the size of the Presidential staff grew as special assistants and aides were added to support the work of the Chief Executive. During the late 19th and early 20th centuries, as the economy became industrialized and the population urbanized, regulatory agencies in the executive branch proliferated to deal with the growing complexities and inequities of national life.

The United States became a world power by 1900, with a consequent growth of the role of the President as a diplomatic leader and as commander in chief of the nation's military forces. As a result, the apparatus of the Presidency grew to meet these enhanced world responsibilities. The world wars of this century proved powerful stimulants to the rise of a strong and often imperial President.

All of this would have seemed impossible during the 19th century. At that time the national government was relatively small and easy for a President to administer. Often the President would have only one secretary or clerk to assist him. Presidents drafted their own speeches and messages and usually had to write them out in longhand. Military commissions, appointments to office, and other documents had to be signed by the President. The only time that an incumbent had any semblance of a staff was when he borrowed clerks or specialists from the various departments and agencies of the government. The President sought advice mainly from his Cabinet, or his "official family" as it was known, and from friends and colleagues in the political community.

As the first citizen of the nation, the President was expected to be accessible to the people. Regular public receptions at

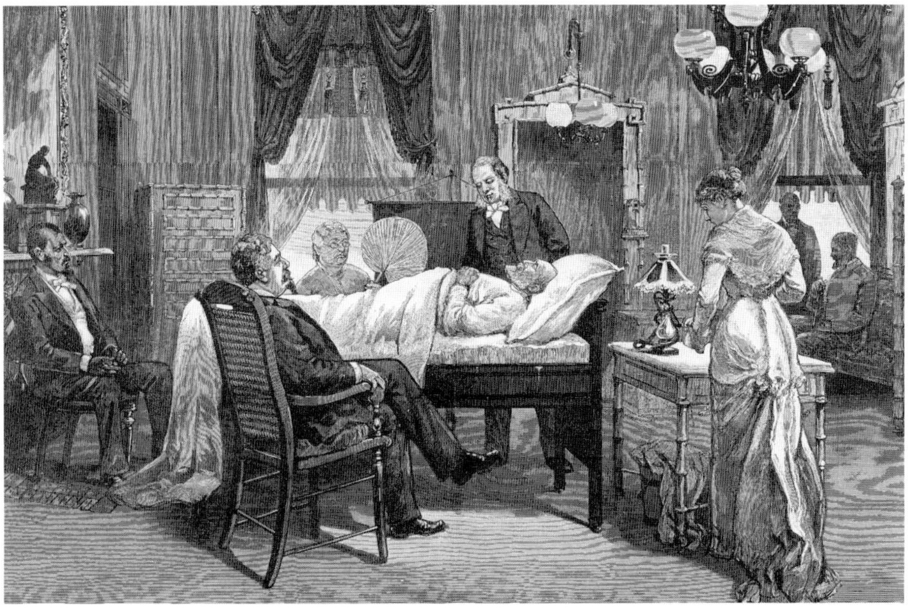

James A. Garfield, shot by a disappointed officeseeker in 1881, survived for 80 days before succumbing to his wounds. Assassins' bullets felled three Presidents before the advent of more sufficient Presidential security measures in the 20th century.

Library of Congress

the White House were common, and the people stood in line to shake hands with the President. A Chief Executive could make speaking tours of the country during his term of office, though Presidential travel was less frequent than in the 20th century. When a President ran for reelection, it was regarded as undignified for him to campaign personally, and no President did so successfully until Woodrow Wilson in 1916.

Security for the President was rudimentary during the 19th century. Abraham Lincoln's assassination in 1865 brought some Secret Service protection for subsequent Presidents, but it was still relatively easy to see the President at the White House during the first three decades of the 20th century. James A. Garfield in 1881 and William McKinley in 1901 were two more victims of the inadequacies of Presidential protection before the advent of institutionalized security procedures.

The role of the President in American political life was less marked before 1900. After the 1830s political parties handled most of the campaigning duties. A nominee for the Presidency would make a speech formally accepting the decision of his party and issue a letter of acceptance that would serve as a major campaign document. After the Civil War, the practice of "front-porch" campaigns emerged. James A. Garfield and Benjamin Harrison began this campaign style, and it reached its peak with William McKinley's race in 1896. More than 750,000 people came to his home in Canton, OH, during August, September, and October 1896 to hear McKinley give graceful addresses that were reprinted the following day in newspapers all over the country. McKinley's rival, William Jennings Bryan, made a "whistle-stop" campaign of the country. Although he lost, the new technique eventually became standard practice in the century to come.

The Presidential campaign itself took some time to emerge. From George Washington through John Quincy Adams, there were no true campaigns in the modern sense. Presidents did not have to be party leaders, and congressional caucuses and state legislators chose Presidential candidates. The candidates directed their appeals to Congress and the legislatures rather than to masses of voters.

By 1828, however, all the states except Delaware and South Carolina had turned to the selection of electors by popular vote. Andrew Jackson in 1828 was the first Presidential candidate to be popularly elected in the modern sense. Further democratization of the process occurred in 1832, when both the Democrats and their Whig opponents held the first national conventions to nominate candidates for President.

In 1840 the election of William Henry Harrison began a practice of electioneering that scholars have called "spectacular politics." The Whigs portrayed Harrison as a national hero who had lived in a log cabin. They used campaign slogans and songs and sought voter participation in torchlight parades. Voter turnout in the election increased. Political parties paid more attention to the popular image that their nominee would present on the campaign trail.

By the end of the 19th century, the appetite for the politics of display and spectacle gave way to campaigns of education that showered the voters with millions of documents and lengthy speeches. The early part of the 20th century saw the rise of merchandising techniques that were borrowed from business and marketed the candidates through advertising and appeals to the voters as individuals. In comparison to the 19th century, the role of the political party decreased in Presidential elections while the degree of popular interest and involvement in these Presidential elections fell off from the high levels of the 1880s and 1890s. In the late 20th century only about one-half of the eligible electorate votes in a Presidential contest in contrast to the 75 percent or more of the electorate that voted a century ago.

Since 1900 the President's political, economic, military, and diplomatic powers have expanded beyond what predecessors of a century ago could have imagined. The size of the executive branch has grown dramatically. The complexities of the office in an era of instant communication require hundreds of special advisers at the White

Presidential campaigns have become a fundamental part of the American political process. This 1880 campaign poster helped push James Garfield into the White House.

Library of Congress

House. The President has become a world figure whose health, opinions, and movements can affect economic markets and political events. Television and radio transmit his statements to the rest of the world in an instant.

Traditionally, until the early years of the 20th century, the President did not leave the continental United States during his term of office. Theodore Roosevelt broke this precedent by traveling to the Panama Canal Zone in 1906, though he did not conduct business with foreign leaders. After World War I, Woodrow Wilson went to Europe for the Paris Peace Conference to negotiate the Treaty of Versailles. Now Presidents can travel to any part of the world at a moment's notice. More is known about the President's views than at any other time in the past. To protect him from danger, the Secret Service has insisted on tight security for the Chief Executive. The result is that the President is better known to the world, but very much less accessible to the public at large.

As the nation's chief diplomat, the President is responsible for the formulation and execution of foreign policy. Through the Department of State he appoints and supervises a large diplomatic corps, negotiates treaties with other nations, administers foreign aid, officially receives world leaders and their representatives, attends international meetings and peace conferences, and makes visits to foreign countries as a kind of goodwill ambassador of the United States. At times of foreign crisis in this century, during two world wars and the cold war that began after 1945, the President has emerged as a leader of democratic forces.

The President must discharge the contradictory roles of serving as the bipartisan spokesman for the American people as a whole while also being the leader of his political party. He makes recommendations to Congress regarding legislation, oversees the economy, assures domestic tranquillity, and provides relief during natural disasters. He is also the chief of state, who participates in a variety of ceremonial activities and embodies the values of the nation when he speaks on its behalf.

To become President and to be reelected requires that the Chief Executive engage in a hectic and exhausting round of political campaigning. That process has been demanding since it became common for candidates to make an active canvass on their own behalf. In the last true "whistlestop" campaign before the advent of modern air travel, Harry S. Truman traveled more than 31,000 miles and delivered 356 speeches during a period of 5 weeks. Public financing now provides the money for Presidential campaigns, but the President has to be the chief fundraiser for his party before and during elections. It has become customary for the Presidential candidate to establish a separate campaign committee to handle the intricate operation of a large and specialized campaign staff.

The duties of the President never stop, not even for an instant, during his term. The press corps wishes to be kept aware

Dwight Eisenhower signs the 1957 Civil Rights Act. Once African Americans began challenging segregation, U.S. Presidents could no longer ignore the racial inequality prevalent in the country.

Dwight D. Eisenhower Library

of his movements and actions in the event of illness or a personal tragedy. His responsibility for the nation's nuclear forces is inescapable, and the mechanism for invoking that terrible option is never far from his side. Should the President become ill or need medical attention, the public expects to be informed about his condition and prognosis for recovery. The activities of his wife (the First Lady) and members of his family receive almost as much attention as the President himself. To say that the President is the constant object of national attention understates the degree to which he is in the spotlight of media coverage and public concern.

This modern expansion of the Presidency would have seemed impossible when George Washington took his oath of office at New York's city hall in 1789. The experiment in constitutional and democratic government that was being launched depended on Washington's willingness to accept the office of President. Support for the new constitution rested in part on the knowledge that Washington would be the first Chief Executive. The first President was an aristocrat, but he approached his new office without seeking to achieve exalted status or arbitrary power. He was devoted to the principles of republican government and was well aware that he was setting precedents. During the 8 years that followed, he defined the institution that the Constitution had only outlined in the broadest terms.

In the process, Washington enabled the new republic to survive its early years. He overcame the emergence of political parties and partisan rivalries, withstood the instability in the fledgling economy, and avoided difficulties with the more powerful nations of Europe. Perhaps most important of all, he laid the basis for a structure of a workable national government. Washington supplied what the Articles of Confederation had lacked: a strong President not tied to the legislative branch but part of the constitutional system. Washington asserted his authority in areas where the Constitution did not specify whether the Congress or the President was to act. Yet Washington respected Congress and maintained good relations with the lawmakers.

The next several Chief Executives—John Adams, Thomas Jefferson, James Madison, James Monroe, and John Quincy Adams—added their contributions to the evolving institution of the Presidency. John Adams's nomination of John Marshall to be Chief Justice of the United States proved a decisive step in the development of the judiciary as a force in national life. The Louisiana Purchase, during Jefferson's administration, doubled the size of the United States and showed how the powers of the office could be stretched to take advantage of historic opportunities. The national political system emerged during this period, and the young republic survived the foreign crises and domestic issues of the years between 1800 and 1828. The War of 1812, which occurred because of disputes with Great Britain arising from the Napoleonic Wars, was the one important military conflict of this period.

The war ended in a kind of diplomatic and military stalemate, but the nation found its independence reaffirmed and its destiny ratified. A fervor of nationalistic spirit resulted, along with an expansion of political democracy for white, male Americans. Black Americans were still, for the most part, enslaved in the South, Native Americans were displaced and persecuted, and women lacked even a measure of full political and social rights. These problems were not addressed as the nation grew. The population tripled, and millions of pioneers pushed past the Appalachian frontier into the Mississippi Valley and beyond. The United States was a growing, more confident nation of two dozen states during the 1820s.

The Presidents from Andrew Jackson through James Buchanan confronted the issues that expansion and social problems presented. The relationship of the federal government to the states, the role of the government in promoting economic growth, the balance of sectional power—all these dilemmas expressed themselves in the turbulent politics of the pre-Civil War era. Added to this mix of concerns was the divisive and explosive issue of human slavery and the fate of blacks in the South. Where did the power reside to

President Warren G. Harding (*right of center*) dines with friends, including Thomas Edison (*left of Harding*) and Henry Ford (*right of Harding*). Men such as Edison and Ford helped to reshape American industry.

Library of Congress

deal with this subject? Were the states sovereign and able to determine what their society and lifestyle should be? Did the power to regulate slavery or abolish human bondage lie with the national government? The President became a focal point for the resolution of these problems as the North and South clashed over the South's "peculiar institution" during the 1840s and 1850s. As the tide of settlement pushed westward, a related problem emerged. Should these new territories be admitted to the Union as free or slave states?

The western influence on the Presidency became evident during this same period. Ten new states in the South and West joined the Union. Andrew Jackson became the first westerner to occupy the White House, and three other Chief Executives from the same region followed him in the next decade and a half—William Henry Harrison, James K. Polk, and Zachary Taylor. American Indians were the greatest losers in the western movement as they were shoved aside and driven into territories far from their familiar homes.

All of the Presidents in these years contributed to the drive to the West and then grappled with the consequences for the slavery issue. Texas was a problem for Martin Van Buren and John Tyler. James K. Polk came into office as an advocate of expansion, which he achieved through war and diplomacy that pushed U.S. boundaries to the Pacific. The aftermath of the Mexican War and the territorial quarrels that ensued shaped the Presidencies of Zachary Taylor and Millard Fillmore. During the 1850s Franklin Pierce and James Buchanan sought to find ways to end the social turmoil that erupted in the violence of "Bleeding Kansas." It was becoming evident that the slavery issue was straining the ties that bound the nation together.

By the 1860s the people of the United States found it impossible to resolve the slavery problem without civil war. Abraham Lincoln and the new Republican Party wanted to put slavery on the road to eventual extinction. The South wanted slavery to live and grow. Sectional tensions led to the outbreak of war, but Lincoln's Presidential leadership helped to preserve the Union and end slavery. After Lincoln was assassinated in 1865, the task of reconstruction fell into the hands of Andrew Johnson. His inability to understand the motives and attitudes of the Republicans of the North contributed to the bitter period that followed. Although the passage of the 14th and 15th amendments to the Constitution represented notable achievements, the nation was not fully successful in providing meaningful civil rights and political opportunity to the new black citizens.

During the late 19th century the United States moved away from the promise of human equality that had been implicit in Reconstruction. Good relations between northern and southern whites were restored, largely at the expense of black Americans, by the creation of a segregation system that would last until the 1960s. At the same time, the nation was becoming more industrialized and more urbanized. By the time of William McKinley's death in 1901, the Union had grown to 45 states, and the rise of large corporations and a modern economy was reshaping American life. The nation watched the achievements of such inventors as Alexander Graham Bell and Thomas Edison and read of the entrepreneurial activities of such industrialists as Andrew Carnegie, John D. Rockefeller, and James J. Hill.

During the 40 years after 1880, millions of immigrants came to the United States in search of economic opportunity. Within the nation's borders, many citizens left the countryside for city life. The general standard of living improved, but the pace of social change brought persistent problems. Children worked long hours in factories and mills. Industrial safety was inadequate, and hundreds of thousands of accidents occurred on the job each year. Pensions, workman's compensation laws, and unemployment insurance did not exist. Labor unions sought to organize skilled workers. The great mass of industrial workers had no defense against the inequities of the marketplace.

Westward settlement ended as the 19th century closed. American Indians were driven onto reservations, and their culture came under assault. The West boomed as prospectors, cattlemen, and wheat farmers

When the Depression hit, Herbert Hoover took a more active role than had previous Presidents in attempting to alleviate the economic woes of the nation, but his aversion to government assistance for the needy proved fatal to his administration.

Library of Congress

pursued prosperity. When the economy faltered in the 1890s, agrarian discontent led to the rise of the People's Party, or the Populists, across the South and West. The return of good times ended that movement as the new century neared.

By 1898 the United States had become a world power. The war with Spain over Cuba produced a dazzling military triumph and added the Philippines, Guam, and Puerto Rico to the nation's overseas possessions. The imperialistic surge ebbed somewhat during the first two decades of the 20th century as the burden of empire became apparent. In 1912 the last of the 2 contiguous 48 states, Arizona and New Mexico, were admitted to the Union. Alaska and Hawaii would not be added until 1958 and 1959 respectively.

During the first two decades of the 20th century, the nation experienced a period of political reform and moral uplift that has come to be called the Progressive Era. Presidents Theodore Roosevelt, William Howard Taft, and Woodrow Wilson dealt with the issue of the extent to which the national government should regulate an industrial society in order to relieve social injustice and promote a more equitable nation. The programs they pursued included substantial changes in the role of political parties and special interests in the making of national policies, passage of legislation to restrain big business and mitigate the effects of industrialism, and conservation and protection of natural resources. Roosevelt and Wilson especially relied on the power of the federal government and the expertise of the regulatory agencies to deal with a wide range of social problems. In time the Progressives also envisioned for themselves a larger world role in promoting a more stable international order. Woodrow Wilson would say that the United States intervened in the First World War to make the world "safe for democracy," but the Versailles treaty and the failure of the United States to enter the League of Nations frustrated his idealistic vision.

By the end of the First World War, the age of reform had passed, and the nation entered an era that President Warren G. Harding called "normalcy." For the first time half the population lived in urban areas. The rise of a mass society and culture also marked the decade of the 1920s. The automobile was changing the lifestyle of the United States, and the infant airlines began a slow process of growth that would eventually tie nations and continents together. It was not, however, a period of vigorous political change. The Republicans dominated the electoral landscape, and Calvin Coolidge was President as the stock market boomed and the economy expanded.

Beneath the facade of prosperity, problems of unequal income distribution, a weakened banking system, and a depressed farm sector signaled possible trouble. The stock market crash in the fall of 1929 began a sequence of events that led to the Great Depression, which lasted until the beginning of World War II. In a 1928 victory over Alfred E. Smith, President Herbert Hoover had been elected as the masterful social engineer who could sustain the nation's economic health. When the Depression hit, his policies did more to combat the problems than those any previous President had attempted during hard times. It was not enough. Hoover failed to deal effectively with the millions of unemployed who needed government assistance, and his emphasis on voluntary action over government programs seemed inadequate for the crisis that the United States confronted. Hoover's grim personal manner added to the impression of insensitivity that doomed him politically.

Historians are still arguing over who was the first "modern" President in the style that has become familiar to the nation. William McKinley, Theodore Roosevelt, and Woodrow Wilson all made important contributions to the emergence of a powerful and purposeful Presidency between 1897 and 1921, but the election of Franklin D. Roosevelt in 1932 over Herbert Hoover brought to Washington a political leader who reshaped the office and the country during the unprecedented 12 years of his administration. Roosevelt's New Deal represented a forceful campaign to find measures that would lift the economy out of its doldrums. The New Deal programs had mixed results, and the Second World War

Since World War II, foreign policy has been the most pressing concern for the Presidents. In 1969 Richard Nixon visited U.S. soldiers in Vietnam; the turmoil and high emotion this war provoked accounts for the continued ambivalence many Americans feel toward the engagement.

Nixon Presidential Materials Staff

did more to revive the economy, in part because so much more money was spent on fighting the war than had been expended on fighting the Depression. In the process, however, Roosevelt demonstrated what a President could do to lift the nation's spirits in a crisis, helped to create the foundations of a modern welfare state, and made it impossible for any successor to remain passive in the face of an economic downturn. The size of the Presidency also expanded as Roosevelt reached out to academics and experts for advice and ideas.

Roosevelt became a world leader as no President before him had done. The economic problems of the 1930s contributed to the emergence of totalitarian leadership in Nazi Germany under Adolf Hitler, who joined with like-minded aggressors in Italy and Japan to threaten world peace. Meeting the challenge of the Second World War led Roosevelt to begin establishment of what has been called the national security state. The Japanese attack on Pearl Harbor on December 7, 1941, brought the nation into the world conflict and fostered the rise of the military power of the United States to even higher levels. Eventual defeat of Germany in May 1945 came at a high cost in terms of lives and resources. The atomic bomb brought the surrender of Japan 3 months later. The United States looked to the United Nations and the doctrine of collective security to prevent another world war and to maintain the coalition that had produced victory.

Instead, a "cold war" between the United States and its wartime ally the Soviet Union began during the years 1945–47 and continued for more than 40 years. The Presidents from Harry S. Truman to George Bush who confronted these challenges found the range of their responsibilities and the size of their staffs continually expanding and becoming more complex. The President of the United States was now expected to maintain peace in a complex and interdependent world while fostering domestic stability and prosperity.

On the domestic scene, the Presidents since the Second World War have relied on instruments of the federal government to lessen the effects of recessions and to keep inflation under control. The Chief Executives have also played important roles in encouraging the nation's development as an industrial-scientific-technological society. One central example of this development is the space program during the 1950s and 1960s, which received much of its impetus from the leadership of John F.

Due to tensions over Cuba, John F. Kennedy's discussions with Soviet Premier Nikita Khrushchev in Vienna, Austria, in June 1961 were unsuccessful. The cold war between the United States and the Soviet Union would trouble Presidents Harry Truman to George Bush.
National Park Service (Special Collection)

Kennedy and Lyndon B. Johnson and landed a man on the moon by 1969. Other Presidents, such as Dwight D. Eisenhower and Ronald Reagan, gained immense political popularity from their capacity to ensure a prosperous and growing economy.

Not all Americans shared in the bounty of the postwar period or enjoyed the full rights of other citizens. African Americans struggled during these same years to achieve their share of the national dream. The 1960s brought urban riots as a growing black lower class expressed its discontent with the squalor of life in the ghettos of the nation's cities. Native Americans, Hispanic Americans, and women articulated similar and other grievances. During the 1960s Lyndon B. Johnson and his Great Society addressed these problems with mixed results, and the struggle for a just and equitable society tested the leadership of the Presidents who followed him. That society remains an unfulfilled promise as the 20th century nears its close.

Foreign policy was the most pressing concern for all the Presidents in the four decades after 1945. The demands of the cold war on resources and lives were formidable. The specter of nuclear annihilation formed an ominous background for every foreign policy judgment. Armed conflicts in Korea during the 1950s and in Vietnam during the 1960s and 1970s produced frustration and division at home. In the case of Vietnam in particular, the wounds from that defeat festered for almost two decades after the actual American involvement ended in the early 1970s. The nation has not yet fully resolved its ambivalent feelings about the war.

Other foreign policy initiatives of the Presidents after 1945 did not produce such tragedy and dissension. The economic capacity and military power of the United States sometimes worked in the cause of peace and hope. Harry S. Truman's Marshall plan helped rehabilitate the economy of Western Europe after World War II. Dwight D. Eisenhower sought a safer world through his Atoms for Peace program. Richard Nixon pursued a policy of détente with the Soviet Union and opened better relations with the People's Republic of China. Jimmy Carter and Ronald Reagan both tried in their own ways to achieve arms control with the Soviet Union.

In spite of all these accomplishments, the American Presidency seemed to be in great trouble during the 1970s. Richard Nixon could claim foreign policy successes during his Presidency, including an end to American involvement in Vietnam, but the Watergate scandal drove him from office in disgrace. Gerald Ford restored some confidence in the institution but was not able to convince voters to keep him in the White House. Jimmy Carter began his Presidency with bright hopes in 1977 but left office 4 years later with economic conditions in disarray and another Presidency that failed to last two full terms.

By the end of the 1980s, Ronald Reagan's rhetorical skill, his personal optimism, and the expansion of the economy contributed to a better national mood and the sense that the Presidency could be an instrument of purpose and effectiveness. However, this renewed optimism was accompanied by a rapidly expanding national debt and an intractable budget deficit. These as well as the challenges presented by the fall of communism and continuing problems in the Middle East marked the Presidency of George Bush, who was unable to maintain the momentum of the Persian gulf victory to win a second election. The new Chief Executive, William J. Clinton, continues to grapple with the problems of his predecessors while facing the new challenges of the 1990s.

For Further Reading

James M. Cannon, *Time and Chance: Gerald Ford's Appointment with History; 1913–1974* (Harper Collins, 1994)

Bernard J. Firestone and Alexej Ugrinsky, eds., *Gerald R. Ford and the Politics of Post-Watergate America* (Greenwood Press, 1993)

Gerald R. Ford, *A Time to Heal: The Autobiography of Gerald R. Ford* (Harper & Row, 1979)

John Robert Greene, *The Limits of Power: The Nixon and Ford Administrations* (Indiana University Press, 1992)

Robert T. Hartmann, *Palace Politics: An Inside Account of the Ford Years* (McGraw-Hill, 1980)

Ron Nessen, *It Sure Looks Different from the Inside* (Playboy Press, 1978)

John Osborne, *White House Watch: The Ford Years* (New Republic Books, 1977)

Roger B. Porter, *Presidential Decision Making: The Economic Policy Board* (Cambridge University Press, 1980)

Public Papers of the Presidents of the United States: Gerald R. Ford, 1974–1977, 6 vols. (U.S. Government Printing Office, 1975–79)

A. James Reichley, *Conservatives in an Age of Change: The Nixon and Ford Administrations* (Brookings Institution, 1981)

Mark J. Rozell, *The Press and the Ford Presidency* (The University of Michigan Press, 1992)

Kenneth W. Thompson, ed., *The Ford Presidency: Twenty-Two Intimate Perspectives of Gerald Ford* (University Press of America, 1988)